You Know You're Over 40 When...

by **Herbert I. Kavet**
Illustrated by **Martin Riskin**
Layout by **CoffeyCup Productions**

©1997 by Boston America Corp.

30 29 28 27 26 25 24 23 22 21 20 19 18 17 16 15 14

Boston America Corp.
125 Walnut Street, Watertown, MA 02472 (617) 923-1111 FAX: (617) 923-8839

You Know You're Over 40 When...

INTRODUCTION

I shouldn't even be writing this book. Most people think I'm only 27 or so. Why just the other day, some girl (ahem) woman thought I was joking when I mentioned the class of 1978. "Middle Age" as you know is anyone ten years older than you and I certainly don't fall into **that** group.

Then again, some college "kids" are starting to call me "Mister." Perhaps that is what started this little guide; someone had to enumerate all the signs that really tell you when You're Over 40 - Just in case you look so young that everyone else forgets.

You Know You're Over 40 When . . .

You feel like the morning after and you can *swear* you haven't been anywhere.

You Know You're Over 40 When . . .

You start wearing Boxer Shorts instead of the "Jockey" type.
You notice colored underwear in the ads but yours are all white.

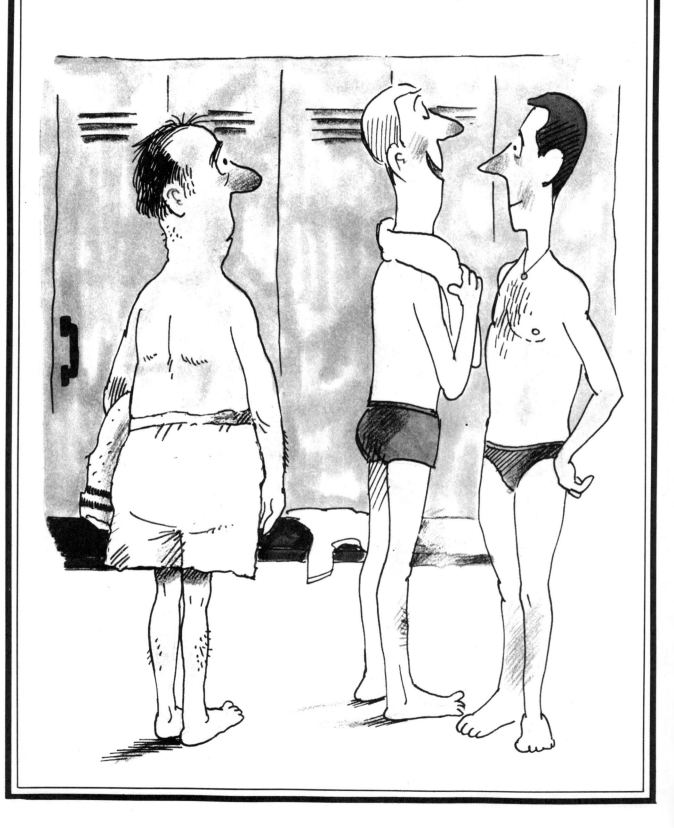

You Know You're Over 40 When...

You meet old friends and you tell each other "YOU HAVEN'T CHANGED A BIT."

You Know You're Over 40 When . . .

You go to a school reunion and everyone looks sooo OLD.
All your classmates are overweight.
You can't believe they have co-ed dorms now.

You Know You're Over 40 When . . .

You learn to control your drinking—you even start doing things that are good for yourself like eating yogurt. You read can labels for cholesterol content.

You Know You're Over 40 When . . .

You start to observe speed limits - you may even pay $10,000 for a restored MG that cost $1500 new when you were in college.

You Know You're Over 40 When . . .

You finally realize that your mother isn't
the greatest cook in the world.
At least she remembers that you hate string beans.

You Know You're Over 40 When . . .

Instead of combing your hair, you start "arranging" it.
There is more hair on your chest than on your head.
Some of your friends grow beards on their chins to
camouflage the loss on the top part of their heads.

You Know You're Over 40 When . . .

Some of the Presidents you actually voted for were later shown to be such incompetents that you are totally ashamed to tell anyone.

You Know You're Over 40 When . . .

You stop to think and sometimes forget to start again.
You appreciate the luxury of a nap in front of the TV.

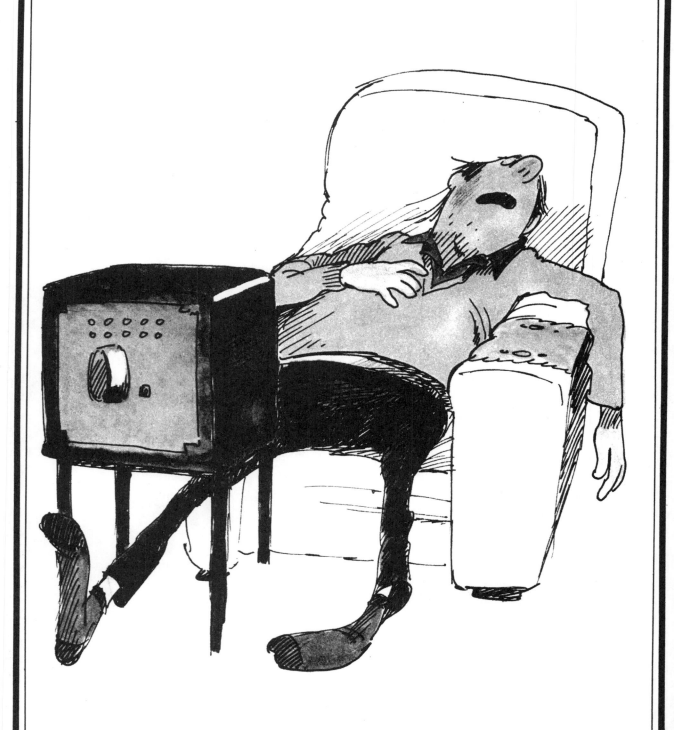

You Know You're Over 40 When . . .

You start entering Senior, Master and Veteran class sport events - and STILL lose.

You Know You're Over 40 When . . .

Work becomes more fun and fun becomes more work.

You Know You're Over 40 When...
Your name appears on every mail order list in the country

You Know You're Over 40 When . . .

You start reading the ads for Hemorrhoids, Constipation, Hair Loss, and various pain relievers. You begin buying the stuff - worse, it helps.

You Know You're Over 40 When . . .

You stop making excuses for sexual malfunction and realize you're tired. You turn out the lights for economic reasons instead of romantic ones.

You Know You're Over 40 When . . .

You start examining your life goals, objectives and achievements and realize you're not making ANY of them.

You Know You're Over 40 When . . .

You can no longer help the kids with their homework. On the parts you help with, they get "C–".

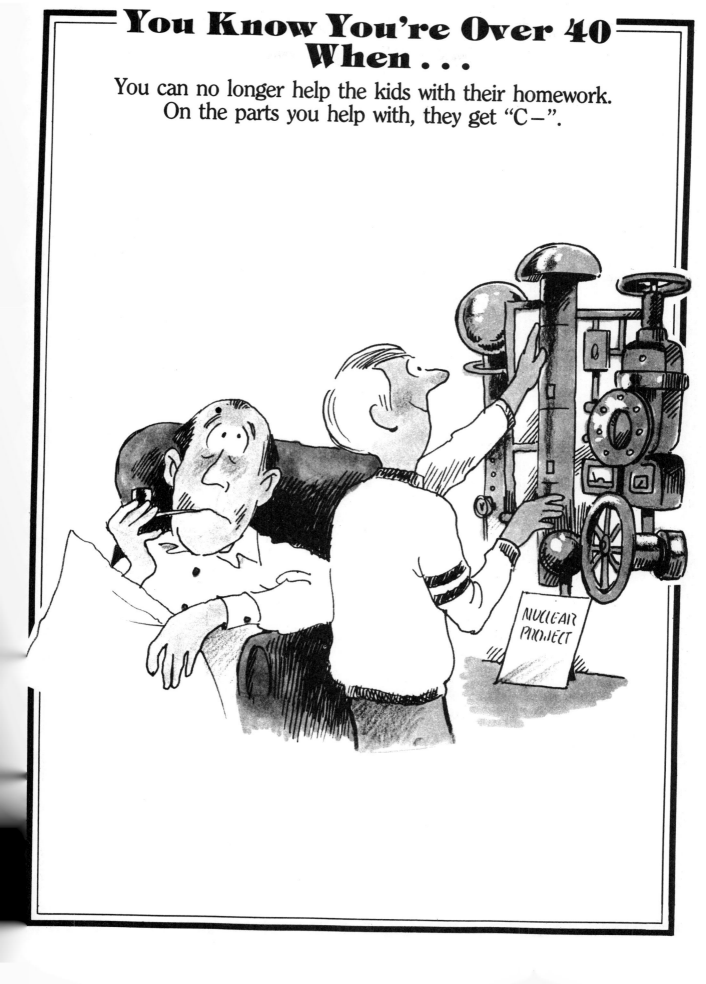

You Know You're Over 40 When . . .

Getting a little action means your prune juice is working.

You Know You're Over 40 When . . .

You start to notice the ages of people in the news like politicians and company presidents - and they're younger than you.
Your doctor is also younger than you.

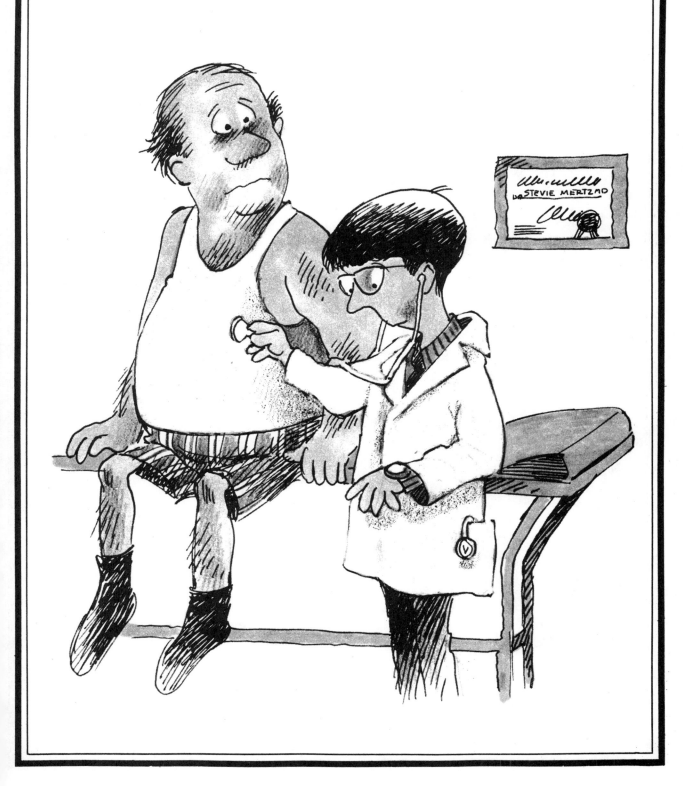

You Know You're Over 40 When . . .

You start calculating how many years you have left, rather than how old you are. You start taking retirement plans seriously. You stop looking forward to birthdays.

You Know You're Over 40 When...

You still feel your youthful ardor,
but only once in a while.

You Know You're Over 40 When . . .

You participate in a ball game on Sunday
and hurt until Wednesday.

You Know You're Over 40 When . . .

Your kids are bigger than you and you start saying things to them like, "When I was your age . . .", that you hated when your father said them to you.

You Know You're Over 40 When . . .

You realize certain foods just aren't compatible with your gastro-intestinal system. You develop a taste for Bran Flakes.

You Know You're Over 40 When . . .

Some of your neckties are wide and some are narrow,
and you can't quite remember the sequence of which width
was in or out and when.

You Know You're Over 40 When...

Your stomach gets upset if you eat raw cookie dough.

You Know You're Over 40 When . . .

You give up smoking because it's bad for you and stick to it for six days longer than when you gave it up last time.

You Know You're Over 40 When . . .

You start to fantasize about career changes, but don't dare make a move. Your boss may be younger than you - worse HE may be a SHE.

You Know You're Over 40 When . . .

College-aged people start calling you MISTER.

You Know You're Over 40 When . . .

You start calling anyone under 30, "KIDS".

You Know You're Over 40 When . . .

It takes you all night to do what you used to do all night.

You Know You're Over 40 When . . .

Your kids start to beat you in your best sport. Then they find excuses to avoid playing with you. You need more time outs.

You Know You're Over 40 When . . .

You find almost any young woman extremely attractive. You can find some physically redeeming quality in any 20 year old.

You Know You're Over 40 When . . .

You realize your contemporaries are
ALL making more money than you.

You Know You're Over 40 When...

You really need a cocktail before 6:00 p.m. In fact on most days, 4:00 would be much more reasonable.

You Know You're Over 40 When...

Professional athletes seem to look younger and younger. So do policemen. You are shocked at the youths in military uniforms that you see. "Why, they're just KIDS".

You Know You're Over 40 When...

You recognize that middle age spread only serves to bring people closer together.

You Know You're Over 40 When . . .

You realize your father was right when he said it's as easy to fall in love with a rich girl as a poor one.

You Know You're Over 40 When...

You're smart enough not to take out all the garbage in one trip.

You Know You're Over 40 When...

You no longer brag about how many parking tickets you have.

You Know You're Over 40 When . . .

Most of your friends are divorced and are busy developing a new life style.

You Know You're Over 40 When . . .

Your kids are big enough to wear your clothes, but they wouldn't be caught dead in them.

You Know You're Over 40 When . . .

You're cold. You start dressing much warmer than younger people. You can't believe "kids" are outside wearing only a sweater and you're freezing wearing a hat, jacket, overcoat and gloves, and you're still in the car.

You Know You're Over 40 When...

You can't remember when prunes, bran and figs weren't a regular part of your diet

You Know You're Over 40 When...

You no longer bounce checks.

You Know You're Over 40 When...

You never owned
edible underwear.

You Know You're Over 40 When...

You remember to stop the newspapers before going on vacation.

You Know You're Over 40 When...

Everybody has already heard
all your jokes.

You Know You're Over 40 When...
You never run out of toilet paper.

You Know You're Over 40 When...

You don't go to
nude beaches.

You Know You're Over 40 When...

You look at the menu before looking at
the waitress or waiter.

You Know You're Over 40 When...

You pay your phone and electric bills before they are due.

You Know You're Over 40 When...

You actually read most of the magazines you have subscriptions to.

You Know You're Over 40 When...

No one cares anymore
what you did in high school.

You Know You're Over 40 When...

You worry about the long term effect
of the sun on your skin, but still love a tan.

You Know You're Over 40 When...

You start to look forward
to dull evenings at home.

You Know You're Over 40 When...

You're resigned to being slightly overweight after trying every diet that has come along in the last 15 years.

You Know You're Over 40 When...

You have trouble finding your kind of music on the radio

You Know You're Over 40 When...

All the prescriptions you never threw out overwhelm your medicine cabinet.

You Know You're Over 40 When . . .

Time passes so much faster than when you were a child.
Weekends arrive quickly, seasons pass one after another,
your kids suddenly grow up and then one day . . .

You Know You're Over 40 When...

Someone throws a surprise birthday party and all your friends come and they bring you gag gifts that poke fun at various parts of you.